My Son,
Not the System's

My Son,
Not the System's

Lynell Lucas

℘

S.E.L.F. PUBLISHING
Simple, Effective, Literary Focusing on Publishing

My Son, Not the System's

Copyright © 2009 By Lynell Lucas

Book Cover Design By Adrian Glover

℘

S.E.L.F. PUBLISHING
4075 S Durango Dr.
Suite 111 #220
Las Vegas, NV 89147
Visit us at www. yourpublisher.org

This is a true story, some names, characters or incidents may be changed or used fictitiously.

ISBN 978-0-9842791-0-4

Printed In The United States Of America

To all who read this book, may you find an understanding in how the Judicial System and the School System works when you have a voice to speak up.

Peace & Blessings

This book is dedicated to Trell and Abey's son, Christian Isaac Ademe-Johnson, my grandson, better known as Scooter.

CONTENTS

Acknowledgements

Chapter

Acknowledgements

Tracy Evans, Thank you for allowing me the opportunity to tell you the story of my son Kentrell. You are my angel.

Raymond Washington, (My oldest Son), Thank you Ray, you were my biggest support. From the beginning you suggested that I write a book.

Kentrell Johnson, (My youngest Son) I am so proud of you and all the accomplishments you have achieved.

Pam Browning, (My Grandchildren and Grandmother), Thank you for helping me find a title for the book.

Coach Mitchell Riggs, (Trell's Basketball Coach in Tallulah, LA.), I want to thank you for putting the heart and soul in making Trell strong.

Mr. William Rogers, (Trell's High School Principal), I want to thank you for giving Trell the opportunity to go to your school and giving him a second chance.

Christen "Scooter" Isaiah Ademe Johnson, (My Grandson, Trell's son), This book is dedicated to you.

Leonard "Champ" Champion, Thank you for being my friend and supporting me and Trell while we were in Tallulah, Louisiana and Las Vegas, NV.

Jaqua Kinta Glover, Thank you for putting the basketball in Trell's hand at a young age. As well as instilling your basketball skills in him.

To My nieces Lora Ann Dorsey, LaTrailla Herring, Lisa Herring and LaVonne Herring. My sincere gratitude to you all for opening your home to your auntie and cousin. Thank you for helping me raise Trell and making sure he received his education. Thank you for caring. I love you all dearly and appreciate all you have done for us. If your father was here he would say "Well done, I am so proud of my girls."

S.E.L.F. Publishing, Thank you for publishing my book. May God forever smile on you and your company.

Turn the Page, (Book layout/editing Company), I would like to thank you—my editor for all the things you did in editing, formatting and turning my manuscript into book form. May God forever shine His light with favor for turning the page.

Lisa Gibson, Thank you so much for taking the time in finding someone to edit my manuscript. May God forever bless you and your family. Thank you for all of your support.

Mario's Market, Thank you for donating to the publishing of "My Son, Not The System's"

Jimmy's Market, Thank you for pre-ordering ten (10) books from me. I Thank you for your trusted support.

Open Book Radio with host Brenda Ward (KKVV.com) Thank you for marketing my book before publication by interviewing me on your radio show. The interview has opened many more doors.

The BJ Harper Show (KLAV1230.com), Thank you for your support by allowing me to tell my story on your show.

Ernest and Pam Fountain, Pam thank you for taking the time to format my book. Ernest thank you for imparting your experience as an author your advise and information is appreciated.

I would also like to thank the Public Defender's Office. Thank you Mr. Randall J. Roske and Mrs. Susan D. Roske for there assistance and hard work in helping me defend my son's character in court. May God continue to bless you and your family.

With special thanks and continued blessings to Judge Cynthia Dianne Steel. You saw beyond the case and looked into the heart of the individual that stood before you. Again I thank you with a humbling appreciation because you saw the good in him and you gave me the opportunity to save my son's life.

Chapter One

My Childhood (Lynell)

I was born in a small town called Tallulah, Louisiana to the proud parents of Clyde Herring and Harrison Lucas. Our home was built on unconditional love and compassion. I don't remember my mother and father staying in the same house, because they separated when I was very small. My father did not move too far from us. He built two houses two blocks behind our house. He lived in one and rented out the other one. I lived with him during the summer and went home for the rest of the year. My father was much older than my mother. He was the one who took me to the Parent Conferences. I was twelve years old when my father got sick and died in July 1962. My sister Dorothy took his death real hard; but I was okay with it, because I was the one who lived with him during the summer months.

I remember my mother sitting out side in a pink rocking chair on the porch. I was twelve years old when my mother told me she wanted me to finish school, and go on to college. She really stressed education saying; "If you get

get your education, that's something that no one can take away from you". I told my mother that twelve years of school was enough school for anybody, and that college is not for everybody. When I turn eighteen, I will be grown and, I will be gone. Mommy would always call me Lynn. She said, "Lynn, I want you to go to college and become a teacher. "

I said, "Oh no, every one of my friends want to be teachers when they graduate."

The next year, August of 1963 my mother died, I was thirteen years old. My parents died a year and month apart. Instead of me leaving her, she left me. What was I suppose to do without a mother? At the time of my mother's death, my brother Dan was twenty eight, my brother Matt was twenty six, my sister Edna was twenty one and my sister Dorothy was fourteen years old. My childhood was very stressful. My brother Matt and my sister Edna raised Dorothy and my I. They did the best that they could do in raising the two of us.

The last words that my mother said to me was plain and clear. But I was just too young to read between the lines. It was a Saturday night. I had company that night. Yes, my mother let me have company when I was twelve. My mother trusted me. She was sitting outside on the porch in the pink rocking chair. She told my sister Dorothy and I to come inside to the bathroom. She wanted to talk to the both of us. She told Dorothy and I that she loved us, and she didn't want us to ever separate; but to always stay together and love one another. She even said if we wanted to go to Las Vegas, we could go, but go together. She hugged and kissed the both of us. She told us again that she loved us. As we were leaving the bathroom, she picked me up; carried me over; and sat me on my boyfriend's lap. She said that I didn't have to sit so far away from him anymore. I didn't think anything different of her behavior other than she was extra nice that night.

Around 4:00am that Sunday morning my mother went into convulsions. Matt put a spoon in her mouth to stop her from biting her tongue. My brother Matt came to the house because he said he had a funny feeling something was wrong. They rushed my mother to the hospital; and she died the next day, on a Monday.

All I could hear in my head was what I said to my mother, "I will be eighteen. I will be grown, and I will be gone." But she left first. Then I started thinking about what she said about education, I took her advice. I started getting more serious about my education. I graduated from Ruben McCall Senior High School May 28,1968. In September of that year I attended Allstate Business College in Dallas, Texas for two semesters. I dropped out of College and moved to Las Vegas, Nevada with Raymond's Dad. Raymond was born February 24, 1974. After Raymond was born, I could really hear mommy telling me to get my Education. I went back to school, attending The Academy of Hair Design, I graduated and received my license in cosmetology. I still felt that I needed to go back to school. So, In June 1984, while pregnant with Trell, I attended Dana McKay Business College, graduated February 1986 and received a certificate in Business Administration/Assistant. I felt much better about myself; after honoring my mother's wishes and continuing my education. I finished what I started. Education was instilled in me at an early age. I instilled it in Ray and Trell. That's one of the reasons I wanted Trell to graduate from High School.

Chapter Two

Meeting Trell's Father

On April 12, 1986, Kentrell "Trell" Johnson was born in Las Vegas, Nevada. Trell was a beautiful baby. His father on the other hand was in and out of trouble with the law, regarding domestic violence charges. That's when the system started with Trell's father. Walter was thirteen when he first went to Juvenile Hall, for stealing a milk truck, and from Juvenile Hall to jail, then from jail to prison.

Walter served seven years for robbing a liquor store, (I didn't know him at that time). I met him in 1982, while working at Gladys' Beauty Salon as a Hairstylist. Walter was next door at the barbecue café. I thought he was so tall and handsome. My co-worker Annie Ruth Yates , introduced me to him. We talked every day. He told me he was living with a lady, but she was only a friend. I told my aunt about him; but I never told her his name. She was pleased to hear that I was involved with someone. One night he called me to pick him up a block from his house. I was to meet Walter at a store on the corner. I knew then that the lady he lived with was much more than just "a lady friend." I told him that I will not be picking him up again. I wanted to know more about the lady. He said that she liked him, but he didn't like her.

We went back to my apartment and had a couple of drinks. We both shared our life experiences with one another. But I felt he was not truthful with his sharing.

We dated for six months and our feelings got more involved. He went as far as calling my other gentleman friend, whom I was seeing. He told him not to call me anymore, because he (Walter) loved me. With our unique friendship, Walter couldn't stand a chance with him in the picture. My gentleman friend called me and ended our friendship, because he respected Walter for being man enough to call him, and for telling him about our relationship.

I finally told my aunt Walter's name. She mentioned it to her friends, and they told her that Walter was married. My aunt was furious. He was not only married, he had also been to prison. Walter never shared any of this with me.

In the summer of 1982, the owner of Guys and Dolls beauty shop asked me to go to the movies with her to see

ET. That evening before leaving for the movies; I told Walter that he could keep the car and that I would ride with my co-worker. But before I left, my aunt called me and asked if she could talk to Walter. I gave the phone to Walter, and she told him, if he didn't tell me he was married and had been in prison, tonight, she would tell me in the morning. Walter didn't share the conversation he had with her, with me.

I went to the movies with my co-worker. The line was so long it took us about thirty minutes to get inside. Before we went in I saw Walter, and he said he needed to talk to me after the movie. I asked him, what was so important that he had to come to the movie theater just to tell me he wanted to talk to me. Couldn't this wait until I got home?

When the movie was over, Walter was waiting for me. I got in the car with him and asked him what was the problem? He told me that he was married, but they were not together. He also told me that he had been in prison. He said if he didn't tell me that night, my aunt was going to tell me the following day. I got so upset with him after hearing all of that. I asked him, if there was anything else he wasn't telling me, that I needed to know?

He said, he went to prison for robbing a liquor store, and that he did seven years. "WHAT!!!" I responded. I then asked him, why he didn't tell me this when we first met? He said if he had told me he was married or had been in prison, I would not have given him the time of day. So, I told him, he had been playing with my emotions, and had heightened my feelings for him. He then told me that he truly loved me and wanted to be with me. I told him I needed time to think things out. He kept coming to my job, calling me, and coming over to my house. He didn't give me the time I needed to think. I told him that my feelings for him had gotten a little more involved, and that I loved him. At least I thought I loved him. So, we decided to work on our relationship.

My aunt was never pleased with my decision; but she said what made me happy, made her happy.

Six months into the relationship, Walter violated his probation. He had drugs in his system. Again, he did not mention he was ever on probation or on drugs. Another down fall. I continued to see him, and I visited him in prison. While in prison he told me over and over again that he was going before the board; and he would be getting out in four months. I believed him. When the four months came around he said that his request was rejected. He also told me (while he was in prison), that I was going to have his son.

I said, "Not living I won't. With your track record of

drugs, alcohol and prison; I will never have a child by you."
And, with authority. Walter would just say "You'll see, you
will have my son."

After that conversation, I stopped visiting him as
much. I started dating one of my clients. Our relationship
was great.

I finally went to see Walter after three months, and
the first thing he asked me, was, if I was seeing anyone
else? I told him the truth. Yes, I was seeing someone else.
I told him I wasn't going to be like him, (holding back the
truth), I'm not going to lie to you as you lied to me. I'm going
to tell you the truth. I was not going to put my life on hold,
because he put his life on hold. He asked me for the name
of the person I was seeing. I told him he didn't know him.
But he insisted on knowing his name. So, I said "His name
is Sam, "Now what! You don't know anymore than what I've
just told you." He went on to say once again, "You are going to have my son." I told him I didn't want to talk about
that.

Again, he told me he was getting out of prison, and
he asked me to pick him up.

I said, "We really don't need to talk about that,
because your four months have turned into two and half
years. So I won't believe it until it happens." It did happen,

he finally got out of prison, in the summer of 1984. He called me to pick him up, and I picked him up. When the guard opened the gate, he told Walter he would be back. Walter said, "No I won't!" The guard told him that the only way he wouldn't be back, would be if he was dead. I thought about that statement, asking myself, "Was he that bad while he was in prison?" I drove Walter from prison to his mother's house. His friends came by and he left with them.

Walter started using drugs and alcohol again, and while high and intoxicated, he came to my apartment and started a fight with me. I remember a time, back when we were still living together; I was home in bed at about 3am in the morning. He came home and jumped in the middle of the bed and stood over me; half asleep and half awake, I was confused and immobilized. All I saw was a six foot three and a half inch man standing over me. He started screaming, "WHERE IS THE NIGGER!!!" I was petrified. I finally was able to sit up in the bed. He then jumped off the bed and looked in the closet, he asked "Is the nigger under the bed?" Then he actually looked under the bed!

"There's no man here!! What's wrong with you? Are you CRAZY?" I asked. When he heard me say that, he went into a rage. He started beating me. When he finished

I was bruised and disfigured. He then took my keys to my car and left. I called the police. When the police arrived, I made a police report against him for domestic violence, and for stealing the car. I was so hurt and embarrassed.

I went over to my aunt's house the next day. When she saw what Walter did to my face she too was angry. She said, "If your mother was here she would tell you that trash needs to be in the trash can. I am standing in the gap for your mother and I'm telling you to put trash where trash needs to go." I was crying as she was saying this to me. I told her I had made a mess of my life. But, she would always have a positive word for me. She would say, "Don't beat yourself up, everything is going to be alright, you just need to make better choices.

I agreed. I then told her that Walter and I were not together anymore. While I was standing outside talking with her, Walter drove up in my car. My aunt ordered him to give me my keys and to leave her property. He did just that, and he left walking. After that, I did not see Walter for about six or seven months.

My sister Dorothy's kid's father (Theodis Glover) passed away. I saw Walter at the funeral. He spoke to me, and we started talking again. He never moved back in with me again. But we continued to talk to one another. He was very nice when he wasn't drinking or doing drugs. He was an altogether different person.

Months after Theodis' funeral, I saw Walter again. He came over and we went to the park, and he put me on his bike. When we got to the park, he started smoking marijuana, and I asked him, if he was going to start tripping. He would always trip out after doing drugs. Sure enough, he started tripping.

When we went back to the house. Water started asking me about Sam (where he stayed, and what kind of car he drove.) I told him I didn't know. He tried to take my keys and take the car. I told him I would drive him where he wanted to go. I didn't know at the time, he was going to look for Sam. We went to the Love Cocktail Lounge. Walter went in, and asked the bartender if he had seen big Sam. The bartender said, "Let me give you some words of wisdom. You need to know who you are looking for and what that person is about before you come in here asking questions. The person you're asking about could be right behind you, and you would never know it; and you could get yourself caught up in a trick bag." Walter looked at the bartender with anger. We left Love Cocktail Lounge and went to the Seven Sea Lounge, I went inside first, and asked a friend of mine had she seen Sam. She told me Sam had just left the club. I felt relieved. When I went back outside, Walter was asking another man if he knew big Sam. The man asked Walter if he was talking about the one with the candy apple Corvette? Walter said yes. The man then said, "He stays right down this street, and his house is on the left hand side of the road.

Walter jumped in the car. I said, "I know you're not going down to that man's house!" Walter pulls up into Sam's driveway, got out, and knocked on his door. It was 3am in the morning. When Sam came to the door, Walter told Sam he wanted to apologize to him for what he said to him on the phone. Then Walter tried to steal a punch. Sam caught his hand and they started to fight. Walter was trying to run a sham. Cars were stopping and the people got out, and sat on the hoods of their cars to watch the fight. I wanted to break up the fight, so when Sam had Walter down on the ground, I tried pulling Sam off of Walter. Walter said "#### you trying to help him Beat my ###!!"

The people who were watching the fight from their cars, were laughing as if they were watching a movie. When the fight was over, I was standing next to Sam. Walter yelled out "I told you, you were #### him! I am going to whip your ### when I get you home."

Then Sam said to Walter, "You better not put your hands on her!" Walter pulled a piece of the iron fence out of the ground, and held it up over his head, and started running toward Sam with the iron pole hollering. Sam didn't move. He told his daughter NieCee, to go in the house and get his gun. Walter was terrified of guns, so he ran in the opposite direction. All the by standers and spectators were laughing their heads off. I got into the car and went home. I didn't know where Walter went. He didn't come (home) to my house. I decided that night, not to deal with Walter any more.

The next day, I went to my aunt's house to tell her what had happened. She laughed so hard, saying "He was hollering while he was running with the iron pole?" And the both of us started laughing all over again.

My aunt became very sick, I had to take her to the doctor. She was diagnosed with lung cancer. She told me to take care of Uncle Red if anything ever happened to her. She died the summer of 1985.

All of My friends thought my aunt was my mother's sister, but uncle Red was my mother's brother.

I applied for a job working at a Nursing Home while still working at the Glady's Beauty Shop. I prayed to God asking Him to give me a Job at a Nursing Home. I would be able to help people here (in Las Vegas) and in return God would bless me. In return my brother Dan would be blessed with someone who would help take care of him. Dan had a stroke and was put in a Nursing Home in Tallulah, Louisiana, our hometown. God answered my prayer. I got the job at the Nursing Home while still working at Glady's Beauty Shop.

Walter and I were still seeing one another. We were intimate and everything was nice, no fighting, no drugs, no alcohol.

One day while working at the Nursing Home, I was getting some clothes out of the closet for one of the patients, my patient kicked the closet door hitting me so hard I threw up. My niece was there, and she took me to the hospital. The doctor examined me, and said I had a bad concussion. I was on workmen's compensation and therapy. My caseworker decided to re-train me for another job, I was no longer able to work in the nursing home. She enrolled me in Dana McKay Business College.

One morning while eating breakfast at a little café next to the school, I got sick in my stomach, and real dizzy. I didn't think too much of it. I just thought I was coming down with the flu. I finally went to the doctor because the problem wouldn't go away. The Doctor ran tests and said that I was pregnant. I said, "Oh no!!! I am not pregnant. Please take the test over." The Doctor said, "No, I don't have to retest you, you have all the symptoms and your uterus is enlarged."

I was devastated, confused, and distraught. The doctor told me I was two and a half months along. I left the Doctor's office in despair. I didn't tell anyone I was pregnant. I went to therapy and as I walked around, doing my laps, I would pray to God for the right answer on what to do about the mess I had gotten myself into.

I went to the Beauty Shop and shared the news with Gladys. Gladys was a mentor to me and a true Christian. I told Gladys I was pregnant by Walter. I was thinking about not having the baby, because I couldn't take care of another baby. I am on workman's comp, and business at the shop was slow. Gladys said, "God will take care of you, Raymond, and the child you are about to have."

I said, "Gladys, I'm concerned with his father's criminal record, compounded with his family's bad history. I don't want a child by him. My main focus is to avoid having my son repeat his father's bad history. If I don't raise him well, and protect him, his outcome would be very negative.

She said, "Don't worry about that, of course Walter will be his father. But your child will be his own individual person." I kept praying to God for an answer, (on whether I should have this baby by this man). I didn't get the answer until the day I went in to get the abortion. When I drove up to the clinic, I parked the car. Just before I got out of the car I saw a beautiful baby. She had on all pink and she was lying on a pink blanket. I looked at the baby, I didn't see the mother, and said to myself, "What is this baby doing here, lying on a blanket under a tree?" When I went to turn around I saw a lady. She was standing right behind me. She said, "Where are you going?" I told her I was going to get a pregnancy test.

She said, "NO YOUR'RE NOT!!, your are going to get an abortion!" I started to cry. She said, "See how you're crying, just think; if you go through with this, how the rest of your life will be."

The lady gave me a flier, and invited me to their facility. She told me she was an Abortion Rights Advocate. I then got in my car and drove off. I thanked God that day for giving me my answer. I went to the facility where she worked and watched a film on abortion. The film showed how abortions were administered. I cried during the whole film. I was so happy that God put that lady in my path.

After leaving the clinic, Walter was the first person

I told I was pregnant. This man was so happy. He kept saying over and over again, "I told you!, I told you!, you were going to have my son."

I said, "You don't know what it's going to be."

I told my family, but they were not pleased about it. But that was okay, I was happy.

Throughout the pregnancy I didn't want to see Walter, I hated him so much.

I went into labor. My sister Dorothy and my cousin DeDe went to the hospital with me. My cousin Ann (Annie Ruth Elliott) and her mother (Fannie Ross-Williams) was also in the delivery room with me.

My baby, was born April 12, 1986. The Doctor said "You have an 8lb - 10oz baby boy." I said to myself, "Walter jinxed me! He said I was going to have his son years ago, while he was still in prison." The Doctor then gave my baby to my cousin Ann. She was surprised and so was I.

Walter came to the hospital acting a fool, hollering and cursing at me, because I didn't tell him I was going to the hospital. I asked my cousin to get security to take him out. After he calmed down, he asked me what was I going to name the baby. I said, "His name will be Cantrell Lucas."

And he said, "That sounds like a girl's name, I want you to name my son Kentrell Johnson." I said "No!" So, he went down to the Vital Statistic's office, and told the people in the office, he was the father of the baby Lynell Lucas just delivered. Walter wanted to sign the birth certificate. The lady and Walter came to my room. Walter signed the papers.

After Trell was born I didn't see Walter that much because he started drinking and using drugs again.

Walter came over to the house the day after Thanksgiving. Raymond (my oldest son) was sitting on the couch, and I was in the kitchen making turkey salad from the leftover turkey we had on Thanksgiving day. He came in fussing and cussing and starting his mess. My sister's kids (Adrian, Ken and Nikki) were at my house. They were so afraid, they ran into the bedroom, and got under the bed. I didn't know what Walter's problem was that day. The telephone rang and he pulled the telephone cord out of the wall. Raymond was about thirteen. Raymond jumped off the couch, stepped over the table and said, "I am tired of this mess! I am going to call my daddy!" and he left. I ran out behind him, with the knife still in my hand; I didn't have time to put it down. When I ran out the door there was a drunk man walking down the sidewalk, he said "The woman done gone CRAZY!, running behind her son trying to kill him."

I was staying in a two bedroom apartment at that

time and I later moved into a four bedroom house. When I moved; I decided to give Walter up for good. This time it was for good. After I had everything moved in, I went out to celebrate. My friend Bea went with me to the Seven Seas Cocktail Lounge. The place was packed. There was no where to sit. I spotted a guy sitting by himself, so I asked him if my friend and I could sit with him; and he said yes. After introducing ourselves; he bought my friend and I a drink. His name was John. We had a great time. John and I danced and talked. Later, before leaving the club, we exchanged telephone numbers. John called me the next day while I was at work. We started dating, and I told him all about Walter. He told me he was not afraid of Walter; and that Walter was not going to bother me as long as he was around. John took a lot of time with Trell. After nine months of dating, he asked me to marry him. Yes, I married John, but I only married him for protection from Walter. I grew to love him later.

I was going to let John adopt Trell, but my son Ray told me not to let John adopt Trell. He said "Trell has his father. I don't like Walter but, Trell deserves to have his father's name." I looked at Ray (after thinking over what he had said) and said, "Okay, I won't." I'm glad I didn't. After Walter's death, Trell was able to get his father's Social

Security. That was a big help in raising him.

On Saturday June 18, 1988 Walter was killed. His attacker shot him five times in the chest. He was killed at 7:23 am that Saturday morning. Walter's father called me at work, and told me about the shooting. I couldn't believe it, Walter was afraid of guns. But it was true, it was Walter.

I went to the funeral but I didn't take Trell, he stayed home, because he was only two years old when his father died. I represented him at the funeral. My friends wanted to know why I was not crying. I told them that I didn't have anymore tears to cry. I cried enough when he was torment-ing me and beating me when we were together. My tears are long gone. After the funeral I took Trell to the family house so Walter's family could see him. That was the last time that he was going to be in their presence. I didn't let Trell go around his father's family. Most of them were dysfunctional and on drugs. He didn't see his father's family until he was in grade school and he only went over one family member's house. Which was Walter's brother Nathaniel and his wife Lois. After Trell grew up and gradu-ated, Lois told me she knew and understood what I was doing and that I did well. She said "You kept Trell away from his family. You did the right thing, because most of them are on drugs."

Now you see why I fought so hard for my son. I didn't want him to travel down the road his father traveled.

The School District wanted to sent an alternative School. That was just a break in the ice. It was far greater than Continuation School. It was the "System." The system is huge, and one you're in the system, it's hard to get out.

Chapter Three

Trell, Birth to Elementary

When Trell started first grade, I put him in basketball for discipline, and leadership. The name of the team he played with was called Bad Boys with Coach Hall. Trell was a point guard. He played four years with that team.

When Trell was in the fourth grade he started playing for the Zulu basketball team with Coach Knox, as a point guard. He played with Coach Knox all year-round, both winter and summer leagues.

I remember the Championship game so well. Ray, Ken, Nikki, Marvin, my sister Dorothy and I were there. Coach Knox had given Trell the play, and Trell hadn't made the play yet. Coach Knox was wondering what Trell was doing. The Coach started scratching his head. Trell looked at the clock, there were 8 seconds left in the game. He began to dribble the ball down the court, until the clock had 4 seconds showing. Trell began to roll the ball causing the clock to stop. Ray yelled to the coach, "Coach Knox

Trell is stalling the clock." The coach grinned, he had already figured it out. Trell picked up the ball and made the shot. The buzzer went off. The Zulu's won the Championship game.

Trell didn't get a chance to play with the neighborhood kids that much unless it was at school. He never missed practice.

My nephew, Ken practiced with Trell practically every day. He taught him how to do his "no-look" passes, and how to dribble the ball without looking.

Chapter Four

Jr. High School

When Trell turned twelve years old his basketball skills had advanced, along with his mind. One day while sitting at home; I asked Trell to bring me my bible. Trell gave me the Bible and I said to him, "Now, it's time to tell you what happened to your father." I asked Trell to read the article to me that I had in my Bible. The article was about his father's death. Trell read the article to me.

He said, "Mom, that's my daddy!", and he started crying. I held Trell in my arms and said to him, "Your father was a loving and kind person. But, when he was addicted to drugs and alcohol, he was someone else. But your father loved you very much." As the days, weeks, and years went by; Trell adapted to the loss of his father. From that day on, Trell learned to love his father unconditionally.

Trell continued playing basketball for the Zulu's. He could only play with them up until the eighth grade.

Coach Knox retired Trell's Jersey (#7), and it read

"From here on out, let no Zulu player wear #7. Trell you have mastered the game at our level. Now go master their game at your level." After leaving the Zulu's Trell played for Bentley Middle School in Las Vegas, Nevada. Again, his position was point guard. After each basketball season the coach gave the team a banquet and presented them with a plaque. The coach spoke about each basketball player. When it came to Trell he said, "Trell out thinks everyone on the team. Sometimes he would even out think me."

Trell played all three years while in middle school.

Chapter Five

High School

In August of 2000, Trell attended Memorial High School in Las Vegas, Nevada. Trell was very happy to attend high school, especially without having his mother on campus. I was employed by the (CCSD), Clark County School District, as a campus monitor. He attended Kindergarten through eighth grade with me on campus. So, he asked me not to follow him to high school; and promised he would do all the right things if I didn't.

Trell played basketball on the freshman team, still point guard. He played very good for a freshman; so they moved him to the Junior Varsity team. The coach was very firm. He made the players run laps if they were late. Trell didn't have that to worry about he was always an hour early for practice, sometimes two hours early. By the time the basketball season started, Trell was on the Varsity team.

They had a Jamboree in November, at Basic High School. The team was so excited to play. The night before the game Trell spent the night with a friend (one of his team players). The next day when I got to the game I didn't see Trell, Jackson, or Chad. I assumed they had gotten lost and didn't know the way to Basic High School. After sitting through the whole game; I went over to the coach, and before I could ask him, he told me that Trell, Jackson, and Chad had been taken to Juvenile Hall. I rushed out of the gym and went straight to there. When I arrived, I asked the lady at the front desk if my son Kentrell Johnson was in detention, and if so, why wasn't I informed?"

She said. "Yes, he's here. But, because it's a weekend you can't see him. He'll be in court on Monday morning."

Again, I asked her why wasn't I informed, why wasn't I called? She said they had called everyone. I told her that was not true, no one called me. I then asked what the charges were. She said, "Robbery with a weapon."

"What!, That can't be true." My mind immediately went to Trell's father's background, and I said, "Lord, NO!, Trell is not like his father."

This is what happened (Per Trell): The night before the game Trell went to spend the night with Chad. They all (Trell, Chad, Frank, and Jackson) went to a football game the night before the Jamboree. They had a flashlight that looked like a gun. They decided to use it on one of their friends at the football game; to see if they could frighten him. And they did. It scared him. He was relieved after he saw that it was a flashlight.

They were all in Chad's mother's car. The four of them decided to go to the bus stop, and pull the same prank on the people at the bus stop. Frank got out of the truck and pointed the flashlight at the people. The people were terrified. The flashlight looked so much like a real gun. Trell then got out of the truck and took a cell phone from one of the people. After taking the cell phone; they all went to the corner store. The owner of the cell phone called the phone, and Frank answered the phone. While he was on the cell phone he said to the lady; "If you give me some money, I will give you your cell phone back." The lady told Frank she would call him back. When the cell phone rang the second time, it was the police. With-in minutes the police were at the store. The officers put them all on the ground. They were all booked.

Chapter Six

Trell's First Court Incident

This brought back memories. My first encounter with the school district was with my oldest son Raymond (Ray) Washington. While at school, he and his friends were passing out fliers for his upcoming show. A campus monitor took Ray to the office to request a parent conference (RPC). When my friend Tony and I arrived, we went straight to the Dean's office, and they told me Ray was affiliated with a gang. Tony began asking the Dean questions, Tony was just as upset as I was. But, the Dean must have felt intimidated by Tony, because he asked Tony was he related. Tony was a friend of the family. The Dean then asked Tony to leave. But, before Tony left the Dean's office, he said, "I will be happy to leave but, before I go, you need to know that if you take a picture of Raymond and place in the gang book or circulate his picture to the North Las Vegas Police Department. Miss Lucas will sue you, your principal, and the Clark County School District; because you did not follow proper policy and procedures.

Policy says, before you can take a picture of any child, there must be a written signed consent form, giving you permission to take pictures. Tony then left."

After Tony left, I asked the Dean, "What made you think that this incident was gang related?" The Dean then informed me it was because Ray had a white scarf on his head. But, at that time there were no gangs with the color white; that is why Ray chose the color white. I found out then that they had already taken Ray's picture and put it in the gang book. Ray was in the 12th grade. His picture would have been forwarded to the No. Las Vegas Police Department, labeling Ray as a gang member. Before I left, I informed him that I would not be stopping here, I will be speaking to the Superintendent of the Clark County School District.

I spoke to the superintendent; informing him that their policies and procedures were not followed. Ray had no signed parent consent form on file, and that was not permitted. Later that same week, the Dean called me, asking me to come in so we could talk about the incident. When I arrived, the first thing he did was apologize. He said, "Miss Lucas, I am sorry for what happened with your son. I too am human and we all make mistakes."

I said, "I will accept your apology on two conditions."

Number one, that you shred Ray's pictures, here and now in front of me, and number two, take his name of the gang book, erasing everything." He said, "Ok", and walked over to the shredder with Ray's picture and shredded it, he then went to the gang book with a black marker, and wiped out Ray's name. The Dean then apologized to me again. And, Ray was back in in school the next day. Raymond was not affiliated with a gang, he was a rapper and a writer.

You can understand how Trell's incident brought back memories. If I can fight and take a stand back then for Ray, I will fight and take a stand for Trell.

My friends and Trell's friends were at court to support Trell. My friend Stasha Westley is a prayer warrior. She asked me and Ms. Cookie (another one of my friends), to go with her into the bathroom for prayer. I was crying so much all I could hear was "Please Lord, Give Trell Favor." When we came out of the bathroom the other parents were going inside the court room. We didn't know who would be called first. As each parent came out, they were crying and said, "The judge is not going to let the boys go." Then, I started crying.

Stasha said, "Put a deaf ear to that, they are talking about themselves."

And I said, "Yes, but they all were in this together."

And with a powerful authoritative voice, Stasha, the Mighty Woman of God that she is, said, "God's going to give Trell favor! Go home and pull his sheets back! He will be sleeping in his bed tonight!"

Trell was the last one to go inside the courtroom. All the other parents had their own personal attorneys. I was the only one who had a public defender. They were a husband and wife team. The Judge ordered Trell and his team mates to write a letter to the people that were at the bus stop and apologize for their radical behavior. Then she said she was going to bound them over until after the holidays.

Our attorney informed the Judge that Trell was an athlete and he had never been in trouble before, and if he remained in the Juvenile Detention Center it wouldn't be good for him. The Judge said, "Okay, I will let him go, and since they were all in it together, I will bring them all back in, and release each one to their mothers."

When I left the court room I was smiling and crying tears of joy, and one of the parents said, "Why are you smiling? This isn't funny!"

And I said, "You are going to be smiling too. The

Judge is going to call you all back inside, and release your sons." The attorneys, who represented their sons immediately went back inside the court room. I was told to go over to the desk and sign papers for my son to be released. I was still crying tears of joy. Trell was released, but with stipulations. He had to see a psychiatrist, take a gun class, two hundred hours of community service, probation for six months, and he had a 7pm curfew, unless he was with a parent. He was assigned to a probation officer, his name was Mr. White.

Trell and I both were on probation. What affected Trell, affected me. I made sure Trell complied with all of his obligations for the courts. The only problem he had was his curfew. He didn't quite understand that he had to be in the house at 7pm. After staying out pass his curfew a few more times; I just stopped him from going anywhere. Of course he didn't like that, but I told him I can't help you once you are in the state's custody. All I can do is visit you and put money on your books. Now that you are in my custody, I can help you do the things you need to do to fulfill your duties to the state.

Trell did his community service and his counseling at the Gus Center. His job duties were to make sure things were picked up and put in its rightful place after each activity. He also worked with the young kids in the game room. Trell and I talked to Mr. Hart. Mr. Hart was Trell's psychiatrist, he was also a member of our church. I told him that Trell had gotten into some trouble, and the Judge gave him orders to see a psychiatrist. Mr. Hart saw Trell a couple of times and then he wrote a letter to the Judge regarding the first incident. The Judge was very impressed with the letter; because Trell had completed everything while having six months of probation left.

The Athletic Director at the Memorial High School, sat Trell and his team-mates down from playing ball for 180 days. But they still had to support the team at the home games.

As time went on, Trell was doing all the right things to get off probation. His probation officer was a good man. On the other hand, my oldest son Raymond, told me not to trust anyone. The Athletic Director allowed Trell and his team-mates to end their suspension early to play basketball. They were so happy. The coach told me   that Trell was going to be an awesome basketball player when he goes to the 12th grade.

Chapter Seven

The Worst Day of My Life

April 23, 2003 was the worst day of my life. I had no idea when Trell came home, I would be facing the same ordeal again. This time it was worse. I got a call at 1:45pm from Ashley Bankhead, a close friend of Trell's. She said Trell had been in a fight, and was being questioned by the police in the Dean's office. He had been there since 10:20 am that morning.

Raymond, my oldest son, immediately went to the school. I met him there. When I walked in, Raymond was fussing with the officer about questioning Trell without a parent present. Raymond told them it is okay to detain him; but you should not have questioned him until a parent was called and present.

Prior to me seeing Trell, the officer made Trell write a statement of the facts and verbally explain what happened.

I met with a male Dean. He wanted me to sign a notice of suspension. I refused, and told him I wanted due process. After the Dean signed the principle's name (who was absent that day), he informed me that I would be hearing from someone in two weeks regarding "due process," I told him it was fraudulent to sign the principal's name without her permission or presence. I left.

As soon as I opened my door, the phone rang. It was Dean Timothy. He told me that we could take care of the due process now over the phone. But little did he know, I knew someone had put pressure on him. I told him that I had to have surgery, and we would discuss the matter of "due process" in two weeks.

The Dean (a male), supplied me with a copy of the suspension report which was full of lies and deceit. There were so many lies in that report, especially the part that said Trell threw the Dean (a female) on the ground. So, I decided to contact Internal Affairs to do an investigation. The report indicated that my conference was with a female Dean. I saw and spoke with a male Dean. I knew then, that I was going to have to hire an attorney to represent my son. I told my attorney that Internal Affairs had investigated the incident and found nothing that their administration or their officers did wrong. My attorney then went to the Juvenile center to get Trell's report. **The report read:** April 23, 2003 Trell had a fight with another student and Trell was taken into custody by the Clark County School Police at 10am.

They had him sign the RPC paperwork. He was read his rights, and then the police officer immediately left the room. Trell was then left in the room another two hours. Trell's mother arrived at the school at 2pm, and requested to see him, and she was denied access to him. Trell's mother was not contacted by either the police nor any CCSD representative, informing her that her son was being held or being questioned by the school police. Again, she was contacted by Ashley Bankhead, a friend of Trell's. Trell was held in custody from 10am to 7pm, without being fed or offered anything to drink. Trell requested some food because he had missed lunch, but his request was refused. Additionally, the officer placed Trell in handcuffs for three hours prior to transporting him from the school. Trell was also present when the officers wrote up their reports and Trell communicated to me that the Caucasian police officer after reading both of the reports, had the Philippino officer destroy his report and copy the Caucasian Officer's report.

My attorney sent this to Mr. Old, (who is over the Internal Affairs Office). Pursuant to the foregoing my clients request is that you re-open your investigation of the events surrounding Trell and the CCSD. Once again they found no fault or misconduct on the part of the officers or the School staff.

Chapter Eight

Trell's Turning Point

Kentrell went before the same Judge who re-leased him the first time he got in trouble. When Kentrell went before her, she said to Trell "I should never have released you." Then she turned away from Trell and started demeaning me.

She said, "Didn't you look in his dresser drawers?

But, when I started to answer her question, she cut me off and told me to shut up; then asked me, "What kind of mother are you, and why didn't you check your son's draw-ers?"

Again, I started to speak, and again she stopped me, and told me to "Be quiet!!" She continued to humiliate me in front of the entire court room. The way she spoke to me was in-humane. She told me I was "A disgrace as a mother." She continued to say, "You should have looked in his dresser drawers!" She then gave Trell thirty days in the

Juvenile Hall while waiting to be sentenced for his charges. When court was over, the lawyers apologized for the way the Judge treated me.

I went to work the next day, and asked Ms. Barr to help me write a letter to the Judge's Supervisor. I hand delivered it to her Supervisor. I never received a response, but when we went back to court I found out that the Judge that sentenced Trell was this Judge's Supervisor.

The only time I saw Trell was when he was in the Juvenile Hall. Trell told me he went home to get a gun that did not have a clip in it. He said that the boy he had the fight with told seven gang members, known as the "Bloods", to come on campus to help him jump Trell. The fight was over a girl, who was dating someone named Jimmy. But she was interested in Trell. Jimmy knew he could not win the fight by himself, so he called in his gang members, "The Bloods." Trell said, during second period, seven of the gang members surrounded him putting him in a circle; but did not harm him because a teacher came out of the office and they scattered, down different hallways. Trell left the campus. He went home to get the gun because he was afraid. Trell said, "Mommy I was afraid, I was just going to scare them."

I said, "Son, you were not thinking, they could have had a gun too. That was a dumb move." Then he went on to say that God told him to get rid of the gun, and to face his fears. So, Ashley Bankhead and a friend took the back pack. They took the gun out, and placed it two blocks down the street inside some bushes. When they checked his back pack, he had two bullets in it that didn't match the gun. Trell was so afraid, he said, "If I get out of this mommy, I will never do anything bad again in my whole life."

I told Trell that God allows you to go through things to get your attention. I also told him that the first time he got into trouble he didn't take that matter seriously. But now you see how your life can be ruined.

While Trell was still at Juvenile Hall I told him, he and I were going to pray everyday at 6pm for God's favor. He said, "But God gave me favor before." And I said, "God will give you favor again, just trust Him." I went to visit Trell every time he was able to have visitors. I believed if I had missed one of his visits, he would have lost his faith. Trell and I prayed as I suggested (I prayed at home and Trell prayed while still in the detention center at 6pm every day.)

The second probation officer and the Dean of the school said, Trell had the gun in his possession at the school; and he could have seriously injured or killed someone. I said, " Please tell me how that could have been possible; when he had a friend get rid of the gun before he went back on campus."

The officers threatened the two girls who took the backpack, and wanted the girls to tell them where to find the gun. These same officers were the same officers who retrieved the gun two blocks down the street in the bushes, and brought it back to the school. They said Trell had the gun on campus. I told all this to the probation officer.

Trell had two probation officers, one for the first offense, and one for the second offense. His second probation officer was nice, so I thought. Again my son Ray said to me, "Mommy don't trust that lady, she is not on your side. She does not mean Trell any good." He also told me to tell Trell not to take a plea or sign any papers. I thought Ray was being mean, but he was right. She would comment on how nice looking Trell was, and how well he dressed, with matching clothes and name-brand shoes. But, she said it in a patronizing tone. I told her Trell got a check from his father every month from Social Security, because his father died when he was two years old. She said she was sorry to hear that Trell's father died when Trell was so young. I also Told her that Trell had a job, and that he worked for Nevada Business during the summer months, and that he could buy whatever he wanted to buy with his money. She then gave me a Dispositional (a report regarding somebody's usual mood or temperament) on Trell. I reviewed the Dispositional report along with her. It stated Trell's hearing date for his sentence, which was May 12, 2003. It also stated that I would have to pay the sum of $750.00 per month to the State for child support. She also said that Trell would be going to Spring Mountain Youth Camp, and his blood would be tested before he left.

I then interrupted her, and said "Trell hasn't been sentenced yet. How do you know this is what is going to happen?" I also informed her that she needed to let the Judge make that decision.

Chapter Nine

Trell Second Court Incident

On May 12, 2003 at 9:00am I was in court with Trell and his Public Defender (the wife of the husband who represented Trell on the first offense). The DA and Trell's probation officer were also there. The Judge asked the DA to state his case. He told the Judge that Trell was a threat to society. He needed to be removed and placed in the Spring Mountain Youth Camp. He also said Trell was a gang member; and he hadn't learned his lesson from his first offense. The Judge then asked Trell for his side of the story. Trell began to tell her about the gun, the gang members, and how afraid he was. Then the Judge said to Trell "I'm putting myself in your shoes. What would I have done if seven gang members would have put me in a circle? Of course, I would have been afraid. I really wouldn't know what I would have done; but you can't take matters in your own hands. You need someone that you can talk to and who could help you with a situation like that." She went on to say, "I see some good in this kid, release him to his mother, and bring him back in thirty days. I will do an evaluation on him at that time." Right then and there, I thanked God for that Judge and for giving my son a second chance.

The probation officer had a look of disappointment on her face. The judge hit her gavel and dismissed the court.

After the dismissal, the probation officer's words to me were, "That was nothing but luck." I told her luck had nothing to do with this. It was all God, and we all went our separate ways.

Chapter Ten

Trell's Transfer to Continuation School

The next day after talking to the probation officer, I went down to St. Louis Street, (another part of the school district) to meet with the board members who were over the Expulsion Department. They terminated Trell's enrollment in regular schools; and said he could go to the Continuation School. But, I kept fighting for my son to stay in regular school. I told them a Continuation School would certainly turn a good kid into a bad kid.

About one month later, I had an appointment with the School Board for the final meeting. I listened to all of them telling me about the "No Gun" tolerance. Trell did not have a gun on campus and he didn't need to be in the Continuation School System.

I've worked with the school system from 1988 to 200l as a campus monitor, so I knew policies and procedures. Even though I was injured in 2001 by a student who ran over me on the basketball court. I was still employed by the District. But, I was on Workmen's Compensation.

A word to all parents: Parents we need to discipline our children more. Why, because, when a child receives an RPC, (Request Parent Conference), there are only a few parents that will take this action seriously, and discipline the child for their behavior. For example, taking their phone privileges away, no computer time, and not allowing them to have friends over, basically taking things away from them that they really care about. But some parents do nothing at all. No!, Discipline is not always spanking your child as they get older. We must use other forms of discipline as stated above. Otherwise, it becomes a vicious cycle. The children will return back to (regular) public school, and start their bad behaviors all over again, ending up right back in the Opportunity School program. I have heard a lot of horror stories from children who have returned from the Opportunity School program. When the children shared their experiences of being at the Opportunity school with me; I asked them if they had shared any of their experiences with their parents? Some shared with their parents and others didn't share with their parents. The children that did not share with their parents, said their parents didn't listen to them. I advised the children to talk to a relative or someone who would listen. I also told them that I would always be available.

Parents we also need to listen to our children, take a stand for our children, and have more structure for our children. The children told me the reason they would talk to me, was because they could count on me to listen to what they had to say. After hearing the horror stories about the Opportunity school, it wasn't the stories that influenced me to fight so hard for my son. I knew my son. I knew the values, morals, and principles that I had instilled in my son, and he was not Opportunity School material. It was the system alone that influenced me. I refused to let the system take a good kid, and change him into a bad kid. And that's exactly what would have happened to my son, if he had attended Continuation School. The System, the Government, and even the President is not fair. So you see, he is **"My Son, Not the System's."**

The School Board made a decision to uphold the decision of the Expulsion Department, and said Trell would have to go to Continuation School and he would graduate with a GED. One of the board members told me that my son had only 4.5 credits. He would only be going to school for six months. He could then graduate and find a job. I asked him who died and made him Trell's daddy. I informed him that he did not have the authority to tell me what my son could or could not do! I told him that my son was not going to work, he was going to college.

After I left there I went to the Memorial High School. When I arrived at the school, I spoke with one of the administrators. I requested a copy of Trell's immunization records and his transcripts. They had no idea what I was about to do. I had been praying about this situation throughout the whole ordeal with my son, I asked God to direct my footsteps regarding the School Board's decision. I needed to know what to do if they denied Trell's return back to public school. The administrator told me I could enroll Trell in the Continuation School via the computer in their office. I said, "Oh no!, I will have him enrolled later, I just need a copy of his immunization records and a copy of his transcripts please." The administrator gave me all the information I had asked for.

After meeting with the School Board, I was told Trell had no more days left to attend school. I then Registered him in the Continuance High School. I asked Trell how did he like the school. Trell said the school really wasn't that bad, and that most of the kids there were there for petty stuff. He also said that most of them didn't complete their homework assignments, but overall they were okay kids. Trell didn't know, out of all the Continuation Schools in the District, he was in one of the better Continuation Schools.

Chapter Eleven

Trell Leaving Las Vegas for Tallulah, La.

After leaving the school, I went home and talked to Trell. I asked him to sit down, I said, "Son, I have prayed to God about your situation, and he told me what to do." Trell listened. I said, "I have lived over half of my life Trell, and your life has just begun. You are only sixteen, so I am going to send you to my hometown, Tallulah, Louisiana. Trell, the south is more of a slow paced environment, and there is nowhere for teenagers to go. It's so slow, you would have to go to the big city for entertainment. Trell we are on a mission. You are only going there for your education; because I refuse to let you go to school here for twelve years and just receive a GED when you deserve to receive a diploma. Your cousins would be leaving in August, (his cousins were here for the summer) and you will be going back with them. I will be there in September."

Trell said, "Momma, what are you going to do with all of your furniture, and all of your things?"

I told him all those things were material things, and they could be replaced. But, he could not be replaced. I gave everything away, except my bed and TV; because I needed a bed to sleep in when I went back to live in Las Vegas.

Before Trell left, I called my niece Lisa, and explained the situation to her. She stepped right in (just like families are suppose to do for their loved ones) and allowed Trell to stay with her. All my nieces were there to help her with Trell. I love them all so very much and I truly appreciate everything they did in helping me make sure Trell received a good education. I told them Trell would be leaving with his cousins, and I would be there in September.

Trell left with his cousins, to Tallulah. Trell was afraid to fly, but I told him not to worry, I too was afraid to fly; but after this flight this would be the only way we would be traveling long distance.

Once Trell arrived, he was not allowed to register for school until he went before the Tallulah School Board.

When I talked to the School Board in Tallulah they already knew about Trell's school situation in Las Vegas. They had the forms form the Las Vegas School District so they already had the records.

During the time he was out of school (waiting for the

School Board's decision), Coach Riggs had Trell practice with the basketball team after school. Coach Riggs was a very good Coach. He not only taught basketball, he taught the boys morals, values, and principles. Coach Riggs told Trell, to hold his head up, and that everything would be alright. Trell went to practice every day until I arrived in Louisiana.

I moved out of my apartment, and moved in with a friend until I moved to Tallulah. I moved the first week of September. After I got settled, I went to the School Board to meet with the Superintendent. I told the Superintendent who I was and he acted as if he didn't remember me. I reminded him while in high school I dated his first cousin. He said he still could not remember me. He did say my name was familiar. I told him that my son would be an asset to the basketball team, and I would volunteer my time everyday at the school wherever they needed me. He said, that would be all good, but he could not let Trell in school; because of the record the School District sent them. I asked the Superintendent how could the School District in Las Vegas have jurisdiction over his state, aren't the policies and procedures different? He said I would still have to go before the School Board, and they would have to approve Trell before he could go to school there.

Chapter Twelve

Obtaining an Attorney

I waited a couple of days, before I went to talk with the president of the School Board. The president of the School Board was one of the teachers who taught school at the high school I attended. He knew my family and he remembered me. I explained everything to him and he advised me to get an attorney to represent me.

I obtained an Attorney, and he said he would take my case. Since he was interested in my sister when we were in High School, he only charged me two hundred and fifty dollars. I gave him all the paper work I had on Trell, the paper work from both the School District and the Juvenile Detention Center. He (my Attorney) asked me to get a reference letter for Trell and he also needed one from a friend to clarify the incident that Trell was involved in. I also had one of the English teachers, Ms. Barr, wrote a reference letter. Ms. Barr's letter read: To Whom It May Concern,

I have known Kentrell since he was in Kindergarten. Kentrell has a strong desire to be successful in school. Kentrell has always been proud of his accomplishments in school. Throughout the years that I've known Kentrell, his conduct has been noteworthy as well as his behavior. He has always displayed a caring and considerate attitude for others. He can readily provide ways to help others to succeed. Kentrell was also a student at the Row Akey Sixth Grade Center in North Las Vegas, Nevada.

At an early age Kentrell, developed a love for the sport of basketball. He has attended basketball camps. Some camps were held in the city of Las Vegas and others were held in Los Angeles, California and other cities in the state of California. Kentell has played basketball on a city team in Las Vegas and he also played basketball in other schools he has attended in Las Vegas. He has been very successful in the sport of basketball. I believe Kentrell Johnson wants to continue to be a productive young man and also become a successful individual in the world in which we live. I also believe that Kentrell will be profoundly appreciative to you, if he's given the opportunity to complete his high school education at your school. Yours truly, Mable Scott Barr.

Ashleigh Bankhead's letter read:

My name is Ashleigh Bankhead and I am writing in reference to Kentrell Johnson and the incident that took place April 2003. Kentrell (Trell) and Jimmy Quest had an ongoing feud that lasted about 3 months. It got worse when Jim was informed that his girlfriend liked Kentrell. Three older guys who were gang members came to the school to help Jim jump Trell. In his defense, Trell got a gun. The gun was not on campus for a long period of time. There wasn't even a clip in the gun. When he had the gun in his possession he immediately told someone to take it. The gun was then stored in the trunk of a car which Trell had no knowledge of. At the beginning of the first lunch, and first lunch started at 10:00 am. Jim and Trell immediately started fighting, leaving Trell with no time to sit and talk. There was no time to do anything. Two campus monitors broke the fight up. Each monitor grabbed a separate boy. The female Dean then walked alongside the campus monitor who was holding Trell. The female Dean wasn't touched or thrown. To my knowledge she was not harmed or injured in any way. I saw her minutes later and she looked fine. By this time the gun had been taken completely off campus to an apartment complex called the Fountains. After school was over I went back to the Dean's office to see if they had informed Trell's mother and if Trell was still there; since I had seen that Jimmy was released. When I got there it appeared to me, they had not called his mother, and the school police was still questioning him. I asked the administrators if they had called his mother, they said no. I asked them if I could call Trell's mother, again they said no. When I got home around 1:45pm I called and informed his mother that her son had been in a fight and was being questioned in the Dean' office. The female Dean later called me, to inform me that I was being suspended from school. I asked why I was being suspended, she said I involved myself when I called Trell's mother. Sincerely, Ms. Ashleigh Bankhead.

Those letters played a big part in displaying Trell's character and the incident was explained with truth.

After the Attorney received the reference letters, he prepared his case, and we went to the office of the School Board.

The School Board called later and gave us a meeting time for Thursday at 6pm. Coach Riggs called and told Trell to wear a whit shirt and tie.

Before The School Board: The President of the School Board opened the floor for discussion. My Attorney made his argument.

He asked the School Board if they wanted to ask me any questions. There were eight members on the School Board, four blacks and four whites. One of the white female board members said, "I don't have any questions for the mother, but I do have questions for Kentrell." Then she asked Trell, "Do you know what type of mother you have? She has lived in Las Vegas for thirty five years and had to pack up and leave everything she had achieved. Do you know what type of Principal you had, in allowing you go to his school? Do you know what type of Coach you had who also allowed you to play on his team and supported you throughout this whole ordeal?"

Trell said, "Yes Mam! I know what type of mother I have, and I thank God everyday for my mother; because when I first got in trouble my mother didn't walk behind me, she didn't walk in front of me, she walked right by my side, all the way through my trials."

When I heard those words come out of my son's mouth I knew he was growing up. I started crying and continued to cry the entire time he was talking. I was glad they didn't ask me any questions.

Trell continued saying, "Yes, I know what type of Principal I had, allowing me to go to his school to get an education, and I won't stop there. I want to continue my education and go on to college.

When Trell starting talking about the Coach he almost broke down in tears, but he kept his composure. Trell continued by saying, "I thank God for my Coach, he instructed me to go to practice with the basketball team, and he has always encouraged me by saying, "Son, hold your head up, everything is going to be alright."

After listening to Trell speak the way he did, I was so proud of him. Of course I was still crying. I would not have been able to speak if I wanted to, because I couldn't stop crying.

The President of the School Board said, "All who wishes to deny this young man to attend our school. Say nay. All in favor of him going to our school. Say yea.

Everyone was in favor of Trell going to their school. After the adjournment, everyone hugged and congratulated Trell, welcoming him to their High School.

I will never forget that night, everyone was so happy, even the Board members were happy. I know God had directed my footsteps to go home, and I was obedient to His Word. He opened up the hearts of man and gave my son a second chance, God got my son back in school, so I give Him all the Glory.

Chapter Thirteen

Trell's first day of School

Trell started school the next day and I started school with him by volunteering my time to work with whom-ever or wherever they needed me.

I thought with Trell's position as point guard, and with him coming from another state in his senior year; he would have a problem with the other teammates on the basketball team, who had been there since they started school. I didn't think they would like him, because they already had a point guard. I was so wrong. All of his teammates loved him. They even said, "We have a real point guard now!"

When Trell was young and playing ball, he would always set the plays up and then pass the ball. He's still playing the same way. Trell would rather pass the ball to another player than shoot the ball himself. I asked him why he didn't just shoot the ball himself. He said, his job was to make the play happen, and the one who was closer to the basket, would be the one he would pass the ball. Trell has a sweet, no-look-pass, and he throws the ball fast. I used to tell him (when he was in the second grade) not to throw the ball so fast and so hard. The other kids will have a hard time catching the ball. But to this day, he throws the ball the same way. He would always say, "They better catch the ball!"

I constantly traveled back and forth between Tallulah, and Las Vegas. One day, Trell called me and told me that some lady (who was at the game), said he and some other boys were going to break into her house. She told someone who worked at the School Board, they told Coach Riggs, and Coach Riggs told Trell. My nieces, Lora and LaTrailla went to the school because there was so much confusion regarding what the woman said. They talked with Coach Riggs and he told them what the lady had accused Trell of. They went to the lady's house, but she wasn't home. But, after all was said and done, it was not Trell who was trying to break into her house. She had the wrong person, and everything was back to normal.

I worked with a lot of good people (during the time I volunteered at the school), including Mrs. Mary Lorraine Jackson Reed, one of my High School classmates who graduated the same year I did. She taught the science class at the High School. I helped her by grading papers and assisted her with her class. One day while in the gym grading papers, as I did on many occasions, on this particular day, I was the only one in the gym. The Superintendent walked in. I said to myself, "What in the world is he coming in here for." That's when he said to me, "Ms. Lucas I want to congratulate you for living up to your word. You told me that your son would be an asset to my school and that you would volunteer your time to the school; and that is exactly what you did, you kept your word." He continued to say, "Everyone needs a second chance. I too had a second chance." I thanked him and he turned and walked away.

I also met Trell's Civics teacher, she was a beautiful and kind person, just a doll. She also worked at the basketball games in the snack bar. She told me Trell was her son, and that she would take care of him. She would put money in his civics book so he could buy food, and snacks or he could get his hair cut.

That's one thing about the teachers in the South, they cared about their students, and they cared about their student's education.

I had to return to Las Vegas for some business. I ordered Trell's Civics teacher a suit. When I returned to Louisiana I gave it to her. She was so happy, saying it was the prettiest suit in the world. She told me that I was a true friend, and true friends were hard to find.

Chapter Fourteen

Trell's First Game in Tallulah

There were about four to five hundred people at the game; and there were no seats to be found, it was standing room only. Everyone was standing outside in the hallways.

Trell was number 5. He was playing and one of the team players on the other team made Trell fall. He was taken out of the game for the rest of the quarter. I got up to go over to see if he was alright and he said, "Momma I am alright you can go back and sit down."

I did just that. When I went back to sit down there was a man sitting next to me talking loud. He said, "Look at those niggers. They aren't doing nothing but practicing, when number 5 comes back in the game it's going to be some ball playing. He will have the game in control, just wait and see." Then someone told him that I was number 5's mother. "He said nice meeting you, we're going to see some ball playing when number 5 gets back in the game."

Trell finally was put back in the game, and the man

said, "Watch number 5, watch how he controls the game. We're going to see some ball playing now!" I just laughed, and I felt real proud of Trell, because everyone seemed to love him, and loved the way he played basketball.

Trell was really proud of himself. He asked me, why didn't I let him go to Tallulah when he was in the ninth grade? I told him it was because it wasn't the right time. The right time was then, right at that moment, because God had directed my footsteps at that precise place and time. "God knows the plans He has for us." Jeremiah 29:11 (NLT)

He said, "I wish I had done my freshman, sophomore, and junior year here at your Alma mater. I love it here momma."

The basketball team was called the Dragons, and everyone saying, Trell was a blue chip by the way he played ball, and for the fact that he was from another state. But, Trell was not a blue chip, he was ball player. I really didn't know what a blue chip was until I asked my oldest son Ray. He told me that a blue chip was a person who was paid money to play ball. I was so stunned! The Dragons held the number one spot for a long time.

One day, while I was in Las Vegas, Trell called and told me to come back to Tallulah, because someone told Coach Riggs that he and another teammate were selling drugs and they were "The big time dope dealers" in Tallulah. I said, "This is ridiculous! Here we go again! Trell was not doing those things.

When I spoke to Coach Riggs about it, he shared a lot of things with me. Coach said, "I know your son and the other teammate is not selling drugs."

He went on to say, that some of the staff at the Jr. High School, was jealous of him (Coach Riggs), because he had taken the team to State several times. He also said that he had championship rings for all of his fingers. The Football Coach couldn't see beyond his jealousy for Coach Riggs. He told me, every year during basketball season something crazy always happened. He said basketball had gotten political, and that the politics had taken all the fun out the game for the kids. I couldn't believe it. I knew in Las Vegas this was happening. I didn't think it was happening in Tallulah.

Chapter Fifteen

The Championship Game

The team went to Monroe, Louisiana to play in a tournament at Carroll High School. My boyfriends' daughter and I were sitting in the bleachers, and Trell came over and sat with us before they started warming up for the game. I told him this might be a tough game because all the kids were tall. They were all over six feet.

Trell said to me, "Momma height don't mean a thing. It's how you out think a person, that's what matters. And I can out think them."

I said, "Son, go for what you know."

We both smiled he joined his teammates, and warmed up for the game. Trell was right, height didn't mean a thing. He had control of the game and he was in the zone. All the teammates played well that night. Everyone was in the zone. The team made twenty one free throws out of twenty two, Trell missed the last free throw. Coach Riggs would practice all night with the team's free throws. Coach would not let them go home, until they all made ten free throws in a row. So making twenty one free throws out out of twenty two paid off. Practice makes perfect, and perfect makes permanent.

McCall won the game 78-56. Trell won a trophy for best offensive player. The shooting guard won a trophy for MVP, and the forward guard won a trophy for best defensive player. It was a great game.

The Monroe News Star newspaper read:

"McCall has been flawless on the floor."

By BRENDA YOUNG

hyoung@thenewsstars.com

It could be a history-making year for the McCall High basketball programs. Both the boys and girls teams are perfect this season. Veteran coach Mitchell Riggs has guided his Dragons squad to a 20-0 record. The Lady Dragons, under first-year Coach John Holmes, are 19-0. The two teams will put their combined 39-0 record on the line today at Carroll. On Tuesday, the McCall boys defeated 17. Newellton 112-62, while the McCall girls downed Newellton 80-17. According to Riggs, it's the first time in school history that both teams are perfect at the same time, but it comes as no surprise. Tallulah has been the home of winning basketball teams. Among some well-known alum, are Lonnie Cooper and Donald Perry.

The Lady Dragons were dominant in the early 1990s, winning three straight Class 2A state championship titles under ex-coach Dennis Chandler.

Riggs has several state championships, the most recent was in 2000.

In 1993, both the boys and girls teams took home the state championship.

Expectations for a successful season are always high at McCall. However, the success of both squads so far is rewarding, led by seniors Rodney Williams, Kentrell Johnson and Brandon Gultery.

McCall finished 24-9 overall and 7-1 in District 3-2A, and went to the quarterfinals of the state playoffs last year. The Riggs tradition is back at McCall, he said, "I feel we are back to our old self."

Photo caption BRANDI JADE THOMAS/The News-Star McCall and Rodney Williams put their 20-0 record on the line today against Carroll.

Chapter Sixteen

Louisiana State Association

I went back to Las Vegas. Trell called me and told me that he was called to the office to speak to someone from the State. I said, "Here we go again." I asked him if he called my niece, his cousin Latailla to go to the school, and he said no. So I called her and asked her to go down to the school and be with Trell as his guardian. When she got there everyone had already left for the day. I asked Coach Riggs why was Trell in the office? He said that someone had called the State (The Louisiana State Association) on Trell, because he was a new student from another state, and the rules were, if you were from another state you were suppose to sit out for one semester. I said, "The counselor told you, Trell and myself, that Trell was good to go."

He said, "That's right." But, the State came into the office, asking about Trell, describing Trell as "The big guy" you got from Vegas to play ball. Coach asked them what were they talking about, and I quote "This little guy here?" Coach informed the State that Trell was not there to play ball. He came for his education. It just so happen, he could play ball, but his sole focus was on his education. No one from the State knew Trell was there, someone had to have called the State and report him being there. But, the counselor gave Trell the green light. It was a big thing with the counselor. Coach Riggs and the Counselor went round and round. So, the decision was made, and Trell was not allowed to play the last game. The school was fined eleven hundred dollars, and they would not be able to go to State. I told Coach Riggs it was a set up. Trell had taken the Dragons to 31 games out of 36, and now at the end, he can't play with his team nor will they be able to go to State.

Coach said, "They are some cold blooded people. They knew that I was going to win State, so they did this right at the end." He also told me all the teammates were upset as well.

Chapter Seventeen

The last game at McCall

This was the last game the Dragons were going to play. Before the game started the teammates were lining up. Most of the team players were crying. As each player was called out they were escorted by one of their parents. This was the senior appreciation parent night. Trell was the last one to go out. He did everything in his power to hold back the tears; but the tears came rolling down as he walked me out onto the floor. As soon as Trell came out the whole gym gave him a standing ovation and the tears really came down then. Of course, you know, I was crying too. The teammates presented the parents with a basketball bouquet and the Coach presented the 2004 basketball gold metal to each player.

After the presentation the last game began. Trell sat with his teammates, and when they went into the huddle, Trell went into the huddle with them. Trell was saying something to them. I was sitting right above Trell, so I asked him what he said to the team. He said, "I told them, physically I am not with them, but in spirit I am, so go out there and kick their butt!"

They were struggling at first, but they made it happen. They did just what Trell told them to do, They kicked butt! McCall won the game, and everyone was so happy they started jumping up and down.

The next day, was a very sad day. The teammates had to turn in their basketball uniforms and bags. The football Coach from the Jr. High School went to the locker room and asked Coach Riggs, "What happened? Why can't your team go to State?" As if he didn't know.

He responded with some choice words and walked away. I knew he had a lot to do with the team not going to state. In fact, he was the reason they didn't go to State.

Chapter Eighteen

Trell's Graduation

There were two months left before graduation. Basketball season was over. The kids were focused on their graduation. They were glad that they were graduating. The big day came, and I was so glad Trell was happy. My oldest son Ray and I returned for the graduation. The entire school was happy and excited. My friend (the Civics teacher) had on the suit I bought her under her cap and gown. When they called Trell up for his diploma I jumped up and hollered, "WE DID IT BABY! WE ACCOMPLISHED OUR MISSION!!! THANK YOU JESUS!!"

As soon as the graduation was over, Coach Riggs came to me saying, "Baby girl, take your son home, don't let him stay here; because you know when they graduate something bad always happens."

I listened and took his advice. I thanked Coach Riggs with all my heart, and told him that I was going to write a book about this one day. I also thanked my family; because without them helping me, we could not have accomplished this mission. I told them how much I loved and appreciated them.

Sunday after graduation Trell came to me, asking if he could stay two weeks longer? And I said, "No, we have accomplished our mission, and now it's time for us to go home son." He didn't question me.

Graduation was on a Sunday. We left that Monday morning, going back home to Las Vegas. We arrived in Las Vegas that evening and Trell was so happy. We put our luggage away. I left him at home to go drop my oldest son Ray off at his girlfriend's house. When I returned Trell was there waiting to talk with me. He told me he was blessed to have a mother like me, and thanked me for everything I did. He said, "I will never forget what you have done for me momma."

Chapter Nineteen

Trell Off to College

𝐈 called around to different Colleges for Trell. I told Trell to decide on which college he wanted to attend, and we would go visit the campus. If he liked it, he could start in September. He was okay with that. He decided he wanted to go to San Jose City College in San Jose California. My friend Frank and I drove Trell to the college. When we arrived, we met the Coach and some of the basketball team. The Coach wanted to see what Trell was working with, so he had Trell run drills.

Trell completed the application process, registering for the college of his choice. About two weeks after we returned to Las Vegas, Trell came in my bedroom with a sad expression on his face. I asked him why the sad face. He said he wanted to go to summer school. I asked him wouldn't he rather wait until September. He didn't want to wait until September, he wanted to start summer school the last of June. I told him, since he had just graduated high school, he needed to wait until September. He begged me to let him go for the summer. I gave in and agreed to let him go. That's one thing about Trell; he always knew what he wanted to do. When he was nine years old he told me he wanted to go to college when he graduated. So off he went.

Trell went to college on the Greyhound bus. The assistant Coach met Trell at the bus station. Trell stayed in the campus dorm at San Jose University until the basketball team apartment was ready. There were four boys in a two bedroom apartment. My ex-husband John and I drove to San Jose and took Trell two twin beds and a dresser. Trell and his roommates got along well.

The first game was a jamboree, and I didn't attend. San Jose was so far away. I couldn't make all of his games. But, for his second game, I drove to San Jose and checked into a hotel, took a shower and drove to the College. When I got there the game had already started. It was three seconds down. I made it there right on time. When I sat down in the bleachers I spotted Trell on the floor. Me being his favorite fan, I started hollering, "Hold him Trell! Stay on him and take the ball!" Trell told me when he went back to sit down, he told his team players "My mother is in this gym somewhere. I can't see her, but I can hear her." He finally spotted me, directly in front of him on the other side of the gym.

They won the game, and Trell received a trophy. When the game was over, I took a couple of pictures of him and myself. To celebrate his victory we went to Applebee's for dinner. After, I drove back to Las Vegas and put his trophy with the rest of his trophies. Trell had many trophies from when he played basketball in the fourth grade; but our house caught on fire, and the trophies were lost in the fire. I had to start all over again collecting them.

When I got back to Las Vegas, I received some sad news. Trell's Civics teacher from his high school in Tallulah, had passed away. She told me when I was in Tallulah, she had cancer, and that she was not afraid to die. I told her she was a strong woman.

I had to call Trell and tell him the sad news. As I began telling him the news, he started crying, he really loved and appreciated her, and all she did for him. We sent our condolences to the family.

Later, Trell moved out of his apartment into another apartment with different roommates. Trell went to practice everyday. He never missed a practice. He often com-plained to me about the coach. He would tell me how the coach would curse at them, and talk down to them. Some of the players would either leave the team or get kicked off the Team.

Through all of the abuse and bad treatment from the coach, Trell continued going to practice and played on the team, fulfilling his obligations to the team, and to the coach.

Trell was red-shirted for one year; because he needed to take classes he could transfer. He played ball for San Jose City College for two years; so when it was time for him to transfer to the University, he would be eligible to play at the University.

Chapter Twenty

Trell Meets His Soul Mate

Trell met his sweetheart in San Jose, California, at San Jose Sate. Her name is Abey Ademe. Abey was with her friend and Trell was with his friend. They all went to the movies together. Trell and Abey would run into each other on occasion. Trell would ask her out, but she always turned him down. Trell kept after her until she said "Yes, we can date." But, Trell would always say, "You are my girlfriend." Trell told me so many nice things about her. I met her for the first time when she and Trell came to visit me in Las Vegas. I told Trell how much I liked her and that they made a good couple.

One day, eleven months after meeting Abey. Trell called me and told me that Abey was pregnant. He wanted my advice and or suggestion. I informed him that it was not my call, that it was he and Abey's call. They were the only two people that needed to make a decision so important as that. And when you both make the decision, it will be the right one. Why? Because you made the decision together. I also told him that having a baby should not stop them from getting their education. You both should continue your education.

Abey's mother decided to let Trell move in with them, and they decided to have the baby. I was very happy about that. He moved in and I thanked Abey's mother for letting him stay there. Abey's father on the other hand was not so happy. He wanted her to be with a young man of their Ethiopian culture. But he (the father) came around. I think he thought Trell was not going to be a responsible dad. He has accepted Trell now as being a part of their family. Trell and Abey had a handsome baby boy. He looked just like Trell when Trell was a baby. His name is Christian Isaac Ademe-Johnson, but I call him Scooter.

Later, the subject of their education came up again. They worked it out. Every family member helped in keeping the baby. The grandmother, the grandfather, the sisters, the whole entire family helped keep the baby while they both continued their education. I love it when family come together, being there for their loved ones.

It's graduation time. Trell graduated from San Jose City College May 23, 2008, and received his AA Degree in General Education. Abey graduated May 24th, from

San Jose State with a Bachelor's Degree in Human Resources and Business Administration. Trell and Abey are still together, raising their son with much help from the family. Trell and Abey are working, but looking for jobs in the field of their degrees.

Chapter Twenty One

Coach Riggs' Story (Let the Truth be Told)

In August 2008, I made a call to Coach Riggs. I needed him to clarify some things for me. Coach Riggs began to tell me what happened after Trell left. He said so many things happened after your son graduated. He said, "Remember the incident that took place in the Principal's office? The High School Association came down to McCall School. Someone called for the Principal to go to the School Board, and someone called for the counselor to leave also, there was no one else left to hold things down at the school except for the school secretary and myself." He continued to tell me that the State, started interrogating my son without a parent or guardian present. They even took Coach Riggs' score book. He said the State thought Trell was in the eleventh grade with one year left to go. Coach Riggs said the State told him that Trell would have to sit out the next year, but little did they know, that was Trell's last year. Coach Riggs also said that the following year they were told by the State that every District game would be played away. Coach Riggs said, out of the thirty-nine years he had been coaching, he had never heard of such a thing as that, but we did it. You had to win all five games in order to go to State, but we got knocked out in the third game. He said that the State had set new rules for the games. They made the school pay for meeting, for food, for their accommodations and for gas to and from the games. He estimated five thousand dollars total they paid out for several different people attending the meetings. He felt the Louisiana State Association was a punishment for him. He said it was a misconception from the counselor. He looked at the wrong game sheet. Coach Riggs went on to say, "If I had known that Trell needed to sit out one semester, he would have sat out, but the counselor gave him his green light, to go." He also said he didn't get enough legal representation. The School District has attorneys and representatives that could have had his back, but no one stepped up. Coach Riggs felt it was done from the inside, he felt that it was some kind of friction; because Trell didn't want to play football. He said, even though it was never mentioned, that's how he felt about it. He felt it was a cut throat situation and

Trell got caught up in it. He felt the local people were trying to hinder him. Again he said, I have coached for thirty-nine years with these kids, it was more than basketball. I wanted to get close to the kids. Basketball was a hook to bait the kids. He said he used basketball as a tool to help the kids stay out of trouble, and so they would grow up to be somebody. Half of these kids didn't have a father, and they would come back, after graduating saying Coach Riggs was a father figure to them. Coach Riggs said his wife asked him to let it go. But he wanted to get his side of the story out. "I wanted the truth to be told. You don't jeopardize fifteen boys, because one guy was not eligible. The counselor was the one who made the decision and he said he could play. If he had told me he couldn't play, I would have sat him down."

Well, it didn't work out that way. The coach allowed the two boys that were not eligible to play football, to play. Coach lost his coaching position, and he started teaching in the classroom. Coach Riggs retired from the school and basketball. He felt It was so much jealousy within the community. Principal Roger retired a year after Coach Riggs left.

After I finished talking with Coach Riggs, I thanked him for clarifying everything and letting the truth be known.

Chapter Twenty Two

Take a Stand for Yourself and Your Kids

My objective in writing this book and telling you Kentrell's story is because; parents need to stand up for their kids. We have to show them more attention, more structure, and listen to them; because they have a voice. And most of all, show them love. Let them be around good people, (find another Coach Riggs). We can't let the system step in and make a good kid go bad.

Continuation School can make a kid so cruel. The School System said Trell was a gang banger and a threat to society. If he was all those things, they made him out to be, he would have no interests in going to high school or college; and basketball would have been out of the question. His love for basketball was embedded in his heart at a young age. I know, because I was at all his practices and all his games when he was in Elementary, Jr. High and High School. Knowing what kind of kid I raised, I couldn't let the system turn a good kid into a bad kid; because he is "My

Son, Not the System's."

As of January 2010 Kentrell Johnson will be attending San Jose State University, majoring in Hospitality Management, with a minor in Criminal Justice. He wants to eventually own his own business.

The Beginning.......

*R*emember They're Your Children Not The System's.

My son *Trell , his fiancé Abey's and my grandson*

Christian Isaac Ademe-Johnson

Domestic Violence

We, as women need to take a stand for ourselves regarding Domestic Violence relationships. If you are in a Domestic Violence relationship get **out!!** Do whatever you need to do to get yourself out of it, and get to a safe place. Domestic Violence is one of the number one crimes all over the world, and 1 in 4 members of a church congregation is a victim or a survivor of domestic violence. *Dr. Rev. Marie Fortune, FaithTrust Institute (1994)*

Hitting does not mean Love. Love is a good feeling, love doesn't hurt, love is compassion, trust, and understanding. So take a stand and get help. If you are in a Domestic Violence situation there is help for you, **PLEASE Call: Safe Faith United, Inc (Helping Victims Help Themselves) 702-624-9641 visit or www.safefaithunited.org**

Email sent to the Clark County School District.

Attention Las Vegas Clark County School Board Trustees, Members and Staff:

My name is Lynell Lucas and the reason for this e-mail is because of an incident with my son in 2003. The result of this incident prompted his dismissal from the Clark County School District. I was angry with Clark County School District at the time because, I felt you let my son down. I felt you should have given him a second chance. I am a Christian and God has put it in my heart to go back to the source. I would like to ask you to forgive me for being angry with you. God let me know that it's not the School Board's responsibility to let any child down including my son or to give him a second chance. 95% of the discipline and structure should come from home, and the other 5% should come from the school.

After listening to my heart, I knew I had to leave Nevada and take Kentrell to my hometown in Tallulah, Louisiana. However, before we left, Kentrell had his last court appearance, and he was given a sentence. I am a praying mother and I'm sure you all are praying parents also if you have children. The Judge told the DA and the Probations Officer that she saw some good in him and he was released to me. That was Kentrell's second chance. I gave up everything, home, car, furniture, and clothes all that I achieved over thirty five years of living in Las Vegas, and went back to my home. I don't know what would have happened if he had attended Clark County's "Continuation School." I was employed as a campus monitor for this very same School District, yet I didn't know once Clark County put a kid in that environment, if they would become that environment or even survive.

The Coach at Cimarron High School told me when Kentrell gets to twelfth grade, he is going to be an awesome player, and he was. He played point guard for the Dragons, and took them to 31 wins out of 36. He graduated with 3.0 GPA and he went straight to College in the summer at San Jose City College. Kentrell graduated from San Jose City College in 2008, and met his soul mate, who is currently his fiancée at San Jose State. She graduated with two BA Degrees. They have a beautiful son. He is a good father and a productive young man.

I would like to thank you for the decision you made, because it made me a better person and Kentrell a better person. I've written a book about the struggles and the journey. The title of the book is **"My Son, Not The System's."** It will be released Early November 2009. I would like to know if you are able to provide me with a contact person/persons, who could assist me in going into the schools to encourage the kids to stay in school, achieve their goals and most importantly, to stay out of the system. I would like to thank you all again, and may God forever give you favor.

Lynell Lucas, Author of, "My Son, Not The System's."

A special dedication to Dr. Linda Young
"WHAT GOD HAS FOR YOU IS FOR YOU"

I WOULD LIKE TO SHARE THIS MAGNIFICENT STORY WITH THE READERS.

In 1988 I started working for the School District. I was working a temporary position as a Clerk Typist II. I was just there until they filled the previous secretary's position. I checked the job list daily for other fulltime positions.

One day, Mrs. McMosley came into the office where I was working. Mrs. McMosley was an exceptionally outstanding and beautiful person, she stopped at my desk often just to talk and check on me. On one occasion she stopped by and asked me how things were going, and I told her my temporary position would be ending in a week, and that I was looking on the job list for a permanent position. They had a permanent position at Row Akey Elementary School.

She said she had been the principal at Row Ackey, and told me to use her name as a reference on my application. She didn't stop there. She also called the school and personally spoke to the principal. Mrs. McMosley said, I needed a full time job to take care of myself and my family.

I turned my application in, had my interview and got the job. Since that time, I have never talked to or seen Mrs.

McMosley again, we lost touch with one another; but I would share this story with my friends. God sent me an angel (Mrs. McMosley) to help me get the job in the School District. As, I went through life, her name would come up whenever someone asked me how did I get started working for the School District.

Twenty one years later, I met Dr. Linda Young. I wrote an email letter to the School Board Members. Before, I emailed the letter I prayed over the email. The board member's pictures were lined up, down the side of the page on the website. I laid my hand on their pictures while I was praying, asking God to let someone respond to my email. Dr. Young's picture was the last picture in the row. I kept my hand on her picture the longest.

I had two responses from my email letter, the School Board Coordinator and Ms. Young. I was trying to make a decision who I would call first. So, I looked at the time I received the emails. The first person who emailed me would be the first one I would call. The Coordinator emailed me at 1:36pm, and Dr. Young emailed me at 4:38pm, I decided to call the Coordinator first; but God said to call Ms. Young first.

In her email she wanted me to call her. She left me her home number and I called and left her a message. She returned my call on a Friday (about three days later). She said, my email was an amazing email, and she had never read anything like that before. She went on to say, "You wrote the Board Members asking them to forgive you, after they expelled your son from regular school. That really touched my heart. I knew you were a Godly woman."

Ms. Young invited me to attend and speak at one of her educator's meetings. She introduced herself as Dr. Linda Young. We started talking and I told her that I started working for the School District in 1988 as a Clerk Typist II for Ronnie Rollback, and there was a very nice lady, named Mrs. McMosley in the same office, who helped me get a fulltime position at Row Mackey. Ms. Young said, "I am Mrs. McMosley." I was shocked. I threw my hand over my mouth saying, "Oh MY GOD!!!!!! The last name through me off."

She said, "I was married in 1988 but I am not married any more.

I was the last speaker to speak that night. Before she introduced me, and gave a scenario about my life. She said, "This lady was working for the School District in 1988 while fighting the system for her son. Look at how God works. He took us around a full circle, and brought us back together again.

I am now working with Dr. Linda Young on a much needed ongoing project. Dr. Young has developed the "Village Concept, It Takes a Village to Educate a Child," She has two slogans I really appreciate.

1. Students are first and everything else is second.

2. In going through a storm you got to learn how to dance in the rain.

Below is his memorabilia.

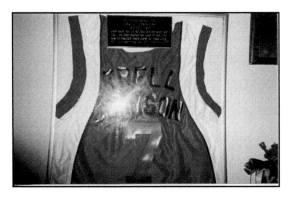

"From here on out let no Zulu Player wear #7, Trell you have master(ed) the game at our level, now go master their game at your level".

The Championship game.

Coach Riggs, located in Tallulah, LA. (Trell's coach).

Trell's principal at McCall Senior High in Tallulah, LA.
(Mr. William Rogers).

Trell's first game in San Jose City College with his mother.

Trell's high school graduation (Trell, Mom, and Brother Raymond).

Trell in the beige pants at his college graduation.

Trell was presented flowers from his fiancé's father.

Trell and his mother at his graduation. What a happy moment!

Lynell Lucas

My son Kentrell Johnson
at 8 months.

Trell and his son,
Christian,

This is Christian and to the left is Ra'neisha, Trell's niece.

Lynell Lucas

About the Author

Lynell Lucas was born and raised in Tallulah, Louisiana. She left Tallulah after graduation and moved to Dallas, Texas. She attended Allstate Business College in Dallas Texas. From Dallas, she migrated to Las Vegas, Nevada where she made Las Vegas her home.

Lynell Lucas attended Dana McKay Business College in Las Vegas, Nevada and she received a certification certificate in Administration Assistance. She also attended the Academy of Hair Design and received her license in Cosmetology. She is also an inventor. She invented a hair product, "The Spike Wrap." She has two lovely sons. Raymond Washington and Kentrell Johnson. She has since retired and is promoting her products.

Scriptures to live by:

"And Jesus increased in wisdom and stature, and in favor with God and man." Luke 2:52

"We then that are strong ought to bear the infirmities of the weak, and not to please ourselves." Roman 15:1

"Remembering without ceasing your work of faith, and labor of love, and patience of hope in Lord Jesus Christ, in the sight of God and our Father." 1 Thessalonians 1:3